GOOGLE PIXEL 7A USER MANUAL

The Ultimate Guide With Tips And Tricks To Set Up And Master The Hidden Features Of Google Pixel 7a For Beginners And Senior's

Andy v. Gainey

Copyright ©2023 Andy v. Gainey. All rights reserved.

Contents

Introduction 1
Features of Google Pixel 7a 11
    Design 11
    Display 17
    Hardware 21
    Cameras 23
    Battery 28
    Software 30
    Specifications 34
Tips and tricks of Google Pixel 7a 37
    Activate Quick Tap 38
    Permit direct captioning 39
    Buying the Google Pixel 7a casing 41
    Start playing now 42
    Register the fingerprints – perhaps two times 43
    Activate Quick Tap 44
    Enable Live Caption 45
    Purchasing the Google Pixel 7a casing 47
    Start playing now 47
    Register your fingerprints - maybe twice 49

Setting up the individual security specifications 50

Check the spam call 51

Adjust your keyboard settings 53

Try the material yourself 54

Personalize the Quick Settings 55

Tap quickly to make the screenshot 57

Multilingual keyboard 58

Turn it off at a glance 59

Allow home screen rotation 60

Enable direct captioning 61

Quickly turn off access to the microphone or camera 62

Making the fingerprint sensor additional trustworthy 63

Tap back to make the screenshot 63

One hand mode 65

Switch off "at a glance" 66

Permit the home screen rotation 66

Wireless charging 67

Speedily go to Google Pay through the lock screen 68

Multilingual keyboard 69

Speedily turn off access to the microphone or camera 70

Now playing history 71
Disable the Google Discover page 72
Display the RAW image switcher in camera 73
Android 12 Easter Eggs 73

Introduction

- During the period of speculations, the Pixel 7a is finally here. As the successor to the Google Pixel 6a, it has some big shoes to fill. The device design itself is the finest that money can buy and is an inexpensive Android device at the previous year appreciations to the influential hardware, outstanding cameras also superior designed, also the 7a appears to have the entire novel level.
- Just you will imagine, the current Pixel 7a got the motivation through the previously Google Pixel 7 likewise the Google Pixel 7 Pro. Google's newest flagship devices are the most good and however,

effortlessly determining the 2023 A-model device to be a budget homemaker. From its Tensor G2 chipset to the new 90Hz display
- While recent A-series installments have pushed their release dates into the summer and beyond, Google is going back to basics this year. This Pixel 7a moved into pre-order at the 10 of May, as Google concluded the important note during the I/O. As for in-store availability, you can also pick up a new smartphone from your local Best Buy — not too shabby. It brings the A-series back to a May launch for the first time since 2019's Pixel 3a.
- Google on their own has come up with few important updates at the Pixel 7a's performance, display, cameras, also charging, and you will pay a little additional in return. Read our freshly baked Google Pixel 7a review to see how Google's latest phone stacks up against Google's Pixel 7, as well as rivals like the Galaxy A54 or the iPhone SE, and whether it deserves to be named one of the best Android By

phone or best. Cheap phones, if not both.
- You can buy the Pixel 7a starting today, with sales officially starting at Google I/O. You will be capable to purchase the 8GB RAM / 128GB storage different via the preferred retailers also mobile carriers, but Google might tempt you to buy it from them in a unique color variant.
- The Google cost is $499/$449 for the Pixel 7a, faintly extra to compare to the $449/£399 you will pay for the Pixel 6a at launch, but still cheaper than the regular Pixel 7 at $599. It is in spite of the circumstance which the 7 also the 7a comes with a lot of specifications as same, which will make them too hard when purchasing for the individual who has additional money use in buying of the device.
- This Pixel 6a is still on sale for $349, therefore when the novel cost is just too big for you to purchase, you will get a substitute.
- Through the similar chipset just like the larger brethren, including the upgraded camera also introduce the wireless charging, the

Pixel 7a will be extraordinarily reasonable in the mid-range marketplace at the current year and could be one of the best value phones out there.
- Just as different Pixel A gadgets, the Pixel 7a comes with the understandable objective at the paper: to offer the high-quality Google Pixel smartphone understanding in just less fund to compare the extra costly brethren.
- With the device, the Pixel 7a is actually a fine smartphone. This comes with the attractive creativity, fine features, also an unswerving camera system also this is just simple at your wallet and you can afford it for only $499. But when the more powerful Pixel 7 offers some notable upgrades for $599 — and last year's Pixel 6a keeps its price cut — it puts the Pixel 7a in a tough spot.
- An A-series phone that delivers all the benefits of Google at a fraction of the cost. This is created through the Google Tensor G2, the Google flagship processor, also Titan M2, Google special security chip, which makes that quicker, additional

competent, with the additional secure.1
- Pixel 7a is designed through a lot of essential features of Google premium phones, now available for the first time on A series phones – such as the Face Unlocking, 8GB of RAM, a smooth display about to 90Hz and wireless charging. The Pixel 7a delivers the basic Pixel knowledge, the price is as from $499.
- Google officially unveiled the Pixel 7a on May 10, 2023, during Google I/O 2023, and it's available for purchase now (no pre-order required). The company launched it alongside its first foldable device, the Google Pixel Fold, and its first Android tablet since 2015, the Pixel Tablet.
- In the US, you can buy the Pixel 7a for $499 at Amazon, making it the most expensive A-series device. This price gives you the only option, which is the 128GB model. When you are living in the America the buyer, you will get the four color selections: Charcoal (dark gray), Snow (white), Sea (light blue), and Coral (pink). The Coral

colorway is merely obtainable straight through the Google, from the online Google Store otherwise this is brick-and-mortar shops at the New York City. The additional three colors will be obtainable through all the retailers, comprising of the carriers

- While Google's flagship phones are widely known, perhaps the most important devices it makes are more understated. The Pixel A has offered to people the models of fine gadgets which is outstanding for their affordability, although run through to a lot of the flagship features.
- The Pixel A-models frequently offers the greatest camera image processing you will have through the device deprived of dropping the thoughtful cash at the flagship. Which was still the issue through the pervious year's Pixel 6a, and this was the risk of being left behind in some locations – inexpensive replacements will be additional to compare to the welcome. The Google Pixel 7a is just the return to the normal.

- Google has used the best parts of the costly Pixel 7 also diluted them, mover over therefore faintly, to achieve a more wallet-friendly price. Is still at the top-level CPU; specifications such as the high-refresh screen also the wireless charging that makes the cut for the initial period; but the major camera have the all-novel, high-pixel-count sensor to maximize detail and low-light performance.
- In the initial look you will think when Google decided to modify other thing at the A-models creativity among generations, and have the Google Pixel 7a at the hands also that instantaneously feel like a classier phone than the outgoing 6a. A recycled aluminum frame now extends over the phone's distinctive rear camera shelf and is almost perfectly in line with the more expensive Pixel 7.
- The shelf doesn't extend very far here, and the display bezels are a bit thicker. The power and volume buttons on the side match the matte bezel, instead of reusing the polished and shiny buttons seen on the Pixel 7. It's not much smaller

either, so you have to be very careful when saying that. Which phone is which?
- The back is still made of polycarbonate (aka plastic) and still picks up fingerprints at a surprising rate. They can be less noticeable in the shades of Sea, Snow and Coral (the latter exclusive to the Google Store) than our Charcoal review unit. IP67 water resistance is welcome, and Gorilla Glass promises quality screen protection.
- You have a choice of face and fingerprint unlocking, though only the latter can be used to authenticate to banking apps and the like. Both were able to recognize us quickly, and the under-display fingerprint sensor is placed a reasonable distance from the edge of the phone so you can reach it easily.
- The screen size and resolution are unchanged from last year, meaning the Google Pixel 7a gets a 2400×1080 OLED panel that stretches to 6.1 inches. That's refreshingly compact in a world where even affordable Android

phones average 6.5 inches or larger.
- The big update is the refresh rate, which now goes up to 90Hz. It may not match 120Hz rivals like the Nothing Phone 1 for fluid motion, but it's a big improvement over the Pixel 6a and its 60Hz display. You can't keep it on all the time because Google dynamically switches between 60Hz and 90Hz depending on what's on the screen. It is also disabled by default, you need to go to the settings menu to enable it. But seeing how smooth it makes every swipe and web page scroll feel, you'll want to take a small hit to battery life.
- Epic contrast and sharp colors are par for the course for an OLED panel, so the Pixel 7a performs well. Natural images and videos have a lot of pop, but still remain true to life. The Natural Color preset turns things around if things are too saturated out of the box, but there's no fine-grained control over temperature or tone. Again, this is a nice, saturated also well-defined just like other mid-range competitor.

- The screen is significantly brighter than last year's model, which already had a brightness-boosting mode that kicked in when you stepped outside. It's not as retina-burning as more expensive alternatives, but we had no problem using it in bright sunlight, and viewing angles are excellent. A flat panel also doesn't have to be content with light reflections like curved glass phones.
- Not much seems to have changed on the audio front, but that's not a bad thing: the Pixel 6a's stereo speakers were great for listening to podcasts or playing YouTube, and the 7a sounds just as clear. The split driver and headphone tweeter lack real bass, but vocals are clear and loud enough. Google wants to sell you a pair of Pixel Buds A-series for personal listening, so you won't find a 3.5mm headphone port here.

Features of Google Pixel 7a

Design

- The Pixel 7a faithfully follows Google's current design language, with a punch-hole display on the front and a prominent horizontal camera strip on the back. This likewise lingers the Google's use of aluminum edge (100% recycled for eco-credits) also thermoformed plastic for the back materials, and will presently be additional resistant to drops appreciation to a new mid-frame. It's rated for IP67 dust/water resistance like the Pixel 6, which while not quite as good as the IP68 rating of the Pixel 7 series, should mean you have nothing to

fear from dropping it in water or dirt.
- Google has expanded the color options for this year's Pixel a-series model. You can pick up the 7a from most retailers in Closet (Black), Snow (White) or Sea (Light Blue), and buying directly from Google also gives you a bright orange coral option.
- As ever, the Google Pixel 7a is almost identical to the Pixel 7. Particularly in the white, the Pixel 7a re-uses the similar matte silver frame, the similar glossy back, dual-camera setup — additional on which below — also flat. Display in advance. When it comes to size comparison, Google's upcoming budget phone is almost the same size as the Pixel 7, last year's budget flagship was just slightly wider, taller and thinner.
- Walk into your nearest carrier and hold the two phones side by side and you'll notice a few additional changes. The camera strap — that signature notch that's become Google's iconic marker for its current design language — is much thinner than on the Pixel 7. This

everything rest on on the Pixel 7a's camera sensor; due to the lesser, Google will decrease the general designs to something extra sophisticated. The camera band also now has a matte aluminum finish rather than the previous generation's primary glass, but unfortunately the bezels around the display remain as chunky as ever.
- What are the things that set this gadget separate from the other of the establishment's lineup? Well, the Pixel 7a comes in two unique colors that you won't see in the more neutral tones of the Pixel 7 series. The blue model keeps with the pastel trend, matching the more muted colors of Google's recent products, while the coral variant looks a lot more vibrant in person than the company's renderings would have you believe. When you desire the orange shade, only know which of the Google Store high-class — no carriers or third-party retailers can trade that.
- The Pixel 7a is powered by the same Tensor G2 chipset found in the Pixel 7 series, 8GB of LPDDR5 RAM, with the 128GB of UFS 3.1

storage. It's the 6.1-inch FHD OLED panel that's finally been upgraded to 90Hz, bringing it closer to the competition from Samsung and OnePlus, though you'll have to enable it from the external settings.
- This device is powered from the 4,385mAh battery, 18W wired charging, likewise the novel for the generation—wireless charging. Unfortunately, Google has limited its device to just 5 watts of wireless power, so you'll want to keep this gadget confined to the stands on your bedside table.
- Of course, if there's one thing Pixel is known for above all else, it's their camera. Google is using a 64MP sensor here along with a 12MP ultra-wide lens, which - fun fact - is actually about six degrees wider than the lens used on the Pixel 7. Used here, it is common. Google continues to cram its images in - up to 16 megapixels here - and while its super zoom leaves a lot to be desired, 1x or 2x photos fits the superiority you will be expecting through the Pixel device. Google in same likewise updated the front-

facing camera to 13MP also, just like the best bonus, backs the face unlock for faster access to the smartphone.
- The Google Pixel 7a sticks to the established design language, using a camera strip on the back to break up the back of the phone. This camera band – according to the Pixel 7 – is higher quality, giving the Pixel 7a an updated look compared to the Pixel 6a. The camera bar on the 6a seemed a little basic, but the Pixel 7a is far from it. Maybe it is created to assure purchasers which is the $50 price label is value that for the ancient gadget.
- Four colors are offered: Charcoal, Sea, Snow and Coral - the latter of which is exclusive to the Google Store. There's no two-tone fun here, they're now monochromatic, with the metal frame and camera band matching the rest of the phone, which wasn't the case with the Pixel 6a. Again, the color of the metal creates a higher quality. However, the substantial IP67 protection remains, so there's no

need to worry about the odd dip or rain.
- The Pixel 7a is smaller than the Pixel 7 due to the smaller screen, but it's thicker and feels thicker in your hand despite being a smaller phone. This is partly due to the flatter display, so there isn't such a sharp curve towards the edges that the phone feels thinner. So while it's probably better for those who don't want a huge phone, you might actually find the Pixel 7 nicer to hold. The Pixel 7a also has a fairly wide border or bezel around the screen, which takes it far from a flagship design. It's also a glossy finish, so it's worth protecting with a case to prevent scratches.
- The stereo speakers stay in place, can deliver substantial sound, and they're well-placed so you're unlikely to muff them no matter what you're doing, so it's good for gaming too. There's also support for high-res music, so if you've got a pair of headphones that support LDAC, for example, you'll definitely be able to enjoy better audio formats. Nevertheless, it didn't

come with the 3.5mm headphone jack.

Display

- The display responsibilities, Google comes with the 6.1-inch FHD OLED display for the Pixel 7a, or maybe that this currently comes the 90Hz refreshing rate. It is the initial period Google will bring in the refreshing rate beyond the 60Hz to the Pixel a model, also although this is not just fast like he 120Hz of mid-range phones like the Samsung Galaxy A54, it's still better than Pixel 6a and 60Hz iPhone SE.
- This could mean that Google's generous battery estimates - more

than 24 hours by default and up to 72 hours of charge with Extreme Battery Saver enabled - may not be accurate if you want to include one of the phone's biggest upgrades over its predecessor.
- This Pixel 7a comes with the similar screen dimensions just like the Pixel 6a, that is 6.1 inches. This is likewise the complete HD OLED display through the 1080 x 2400 resolution, 20:9 aspect ratio also comes with the Corning Gorilla Glass 3 for durability. Nevertheless, Google has design some slight enhancements to make the Pixel 7a a slight the best.
- With an increased screen refresh rate, you can expect smoother scrolling, animations and better graphics while playing. Nevertheless, the Smooth Display setting is incapacitated through the default, therefore you get to allow it manually. This is probably due to the Pixel 7a's lower battery life (higher refresh rate reduces battery life), which we'll get to in a bit.
- At the interior, Google packed the innovative Tensor G2 chip that is the enhancement above the initial -

generation Tensor in the Pixel 6a. You likewise have the 8GB of RAM (the 6a only had 6GB), but moreover, the only storage selection is 128GB.
- On paper, the Pixel 7a's specs look really impressive for a phone in this price range, but it's not a terribly big upgrade from what you can get with the Pixel 6a. Yes, the 90Hz refresh rate definitely helps, but I feel like it might not be that noticeable to most people who want an affordable budget phone, as the Pixel 6a is still a good buy. And the extra RAM helps, but it's still pretty insignificant in day-to-day use
- You'll also be impressed by how quickly the cameras can capture a scene. You used the Pixel 7a to take photos of my toddler who can barely sit or stand (other parents understand my plight, right?), and the resulting images turned out beautifully. The Tensor G2 really helps the Pixel 7a shoot fast.
- The Pixel 7a display story is interesting as little has changed compared to the Pixel 6a except for a change in refresh rate. The move

to 90Hz means you'll get smoother scrolling through your apps, boost the spec sheet on an older phone, and help make it more competitive against the competition. You will choose for 60Hz, and many people will prefer the 90Hz also choose to use it. No adaptive upgrade option.
- But otherwise it's a good quality display, with full HD resolution that's true to size to give nice detail, with good color saturation so it's nice and vibrant. Setting it up with the Pixel 7 Pro isn't quite as bright, and there are times when it looks a little dull, more apparent in daylight than in dark situations at the place of absence of the peak brightness is lesser significant.
- There's enough brightness to deliver HDR visuals, and on balance, it's hard to criticize this display too much at this price, though if it's brightness you're after, you might find Samsung's Galaxy A54 a better choice when it comes to display. .
- Under the display is a fingerprint scanner that opens quickly and you'll find it reliable enough for everyday use. It supports face

unlock, but as was the case with the Pixel 7 models, face unlock appears to only be used to unlock the device — it doesn't extend to unlocking other apps on your phone. Still, it's a faster way to log into your device when you're looking at it.

Hardware

- Among the major captions for the device which is it uses the similar Tensor G2 hardware just like the Google's flagship device, the Pixel 7 Pro (and the Pixel 7 for which matter). Certainly, this is the similar hardware Google is using at the Pixel Tablet also in the Pixel Fold, therefore you will say you are having much for the money.
- The advantage of having higher-end hardware is that it supports all

the features you get elsewhere. These little details like hi-res audio support, AI and all things Google mean there aren't many compromises when choosing a mid-range device. Of a truth, this is the extra costly package presently to compare if Google dragged the guideline through the Pixel 6a, and there are some establishments which gives the class of hardware in this phone position; This was one of the strengths of the iPhone SE, although Apple's cheaper phone is hampered by an old design and lack of some features. Sure, there's only 8GB of RAM and only one storage option, but otherwise, the hardware gives you a lot.

- There's a 4,385mAh battery, plus wireless charging, so it's a great opportunity to grab a wireless charger for your Pixel. This will be popular with those who want that kind of convenience but don't have wireless charging like you'll find on the Pixel 7 Pro. The wired charging speed is 18W, not very fast, or 7.5W wireless, which again is not very fast, and this is one area where some competitors will have an advantage, giving you faster charging speeds. Battery life is good, with the Pixel 7a easily getting through a typical day.

Cameras

- The Pixel 7a comes with the good - sounding 64MP major camera, according to Google is 72% bigger to compare the Pixel 6a's 12MP major camera. It's also the highest-resolution camera seen on a Pixel to date, beating the 50MP sensor seen on the Pixel 7 and Pixel 7 Pro.
- It is joined by an upgraded 13MP ultra-wide camera and a front-facing 13MP selfie camera. All three of these cameras are capable of 4K video, with 60fps for the main camera and 30fps for ultra-wide and selfies.
- There's no zoom camera (as is typical for phones in this price

range), but Google does boast an updated Super Res Zoom for the Pixel 7a. Thanks to the 64 megapixel sensor, you will be able to zoom in effectively by 8x.
- Add to that Google's excellent photography software toolbox, packed with handy features like Photo Unblur and Magic Eraser, plus a new long exposure mode for expertly blurred shots. Night Sight, Google lower-light mode, is likewise back also is said to be twofold just faster also sharp just like the Pixel 6a's type.
- Although the Pixel 7a is the budget phone in the Pixel 7 line, Google decided to give it some impressive camera hardware - even surpassing the Pixel 7 and Pixel 7 Pro in some aspects.
- The Pixel 7a has the 64-megapixel major camera and a 13-megapixel ultra-wide sensor. In comparison, the Pixel 7 and Pixel 7 Pro both have a 50MP main camera and a 12MP ultra-wide camera. However, Google claims that while the Pixel 7a has a higher megapixel count than its sibling, the sensor isn't as big as the one on the Pixel 7 and 7

Pro. This means that the Pixel 7a might not be as good when it comes to taking low-light pictures.
- With the Google Pixel 6a, you could already take great photos without much effort, and that was just with the reliable 12MP camera. Although working through the Pixel 7a, I'm actually overwhelmed through the image superiority. The 64MP camera is ridiculous because it takes incredibly detailed and sharp photos without over-processing.
- The Pixel 7a has a dual-camera system at the behind through the major camera and an ultra-wide camera, while the 7a lacks optical zoom. It's also not the same camera you'll find in the Pixel 7 or Pixel 7 Pro, which have a 50-megapixel main sensor compared to the 64-megapixel sensor used here. Don't fall into the trap of thinking that more megapixels automatically make for a better camera, as not all sensors are created equal.
- However, it's also a complete change from the Pixel 6a in terms of hardware. This is new ground for Google, which has been pretty

consistent with its Pixel phone cameras for several years. The bottom line, though, is that it's a Pixel camera, so it's not just about the optics and sensors, but the processing that happens after you press the shutter button.
- The ultra-wide camera gives you creative options and the performance is good enough, but it's something to consider. Not because the ultra-wide lens is bad, but because the lens switching controls aren't as smooth as we'd like. When you use ultra-wide and switch to the main camera, it doesn't instantly switch to another lens. Instead, it cuts out the ultra-wide sensor to give you a pristine view. Unfortunately, if you're too quick to take a shot, you'll be taking that shot from the cropped ultra-wide sensor - and it's possible that subsequent zoomed-in photos will come from that sensor as well.
- And there's a big difference in the quality you get from the ultrawide and the main camera - especially when it comes to zooming. So just be careful when switching from the ultra-wide to the main camera and

zoom - you'll see a small pulse on the screen when switching cameras, and there's a good chance Google will fix this with a software update.
- Otherwise, the Pixel delivers on the strengths we've come to expect from a Pixel camera. The main sensor copes well in almost all conditions, takes adept low-light and night shots, and also delivers excellent portrait images. Edge detection is excellent, processing only takes a second when you flip to view your shot. Night vision is still the greatest skill - not continuously up to the similarity of the cost, also presently faster to compare on the Pixel 6a.
- A hybrid zoom system can also use Google's computational photography to sharpen images. The results are usable (as long as their range isn't too large), but they can't compete with a camera packed in a proper zoom lens.
- It's not just about taking those pictures, but what happens after them, with Google Photos options to apply Magic Eraser or camouflage elements to photos,

add background blur, and more. As a complete package - a flaw we believe needs to be addressed - the Pixel 7a replicates Google's excellence in delivering a great camera in every situation. Truth be told, it didn't come with zoom, and at the pricing place, this is extremely competitive also among of the greatest in every round packages at the market place.

Battery

- Stuff under the hood of the Pixel 7a is the same Tensor G2 chipset from the Pixel 7 series. It's paired with 8GB of RAM (another first) and 128GB of storage, which is comparable to rival phones. Optimistically the Tensor chip will likewise offer extraordinary notches for a mid-range device,

such phones at this price point (excluding the iPhone SE) use pretty anemic chips. It might even be able to beat the Pixel 7, based on the estimated pre-release results.
- If the Pixel is in short of battery, you will be capable to add it up via the wired adapter up to 18W, otherwise through the 7.5W wireless charging, additional initial for Pixel a-series phones.
- The battery capacity inside the Pixel 7a is 4385 mAh. That makes it slightly larger than the Pixel 7's 4,355 mAh battery. This difference is likely to be insignificant in the end.
- You can charge this battery with a USB-C cable at 18W. That's slower than the Pixel 7's wired charging speed, but only by 2 watts (again, negligible). Just through every current Pixels, the Pixel 7a do not come with the charger at the box, therefore you will desire to buy the smartphone charger otherwise using the one you previously have.
- At the initial period in the A models, the Pixel 7a backs wireless charging. It's slow at just 7.5W, but

- it will work with any Qi-compatible wireless charger you'll find.
- Unfortunately, the Pixel 7a doesn't support battery sharing, which is the wireless charging feature of the Pixel line. This means you won't be able to draw power from the Pixel 7a to charge your headphones, smartwatch, or other accessories.

Software

- The Pixel device will not be the Pixel deprived of high-class Android specifications, also truth be told the Pixel 7a gives the specifications you will imagine, such Call Assist, Clear Calling and Direct My Call. You will just need security, it comes with an under-display fingerprint opening, alongside via the Face opening for included suitability such as the

Pixel 7. You are certain additional Pixel-only specifications in the forthcoming, appreciation to Google's in upcoming Drop upgrades.
- At this point, if you've used the latest Pixel phone, you probably know what to expect when it comes to hardware. Not like the legacy Nexus devices, the Pixel models offers the totally exceptional take at the Android which centers at the neat aesthetics also gives the host of AI-powered apparatuses also specifications. The Pixel 7a bucks that trend and promises the same experience you love from the Pixel 7 series at a lower price. Google also guarantees the same level of support as its flagships, with three major operating system updates starting with Android 14 later this year.
- You'll get Android 13 with both the Pixel 7a and the Pixel 7 and Pixel 7 Pro. Also, like the standard Pixel 7 line, the Pixel 7a will receive three years of OS upgrades with five years of security patches.
- At this point, Android 13 is pretty mature and Android 14 is on the

horizon. Android 13 is the first version of Android I've really dug into, and I enjoyed it quite a bit on the Pixel 7a – especially since it's a "clean" version of Android without the various manufacturer layers.

- Android 13, without any custom forks, is simple and clean. Most individual are huge admirer of Google's Material You theme engine due to it aids you in personalizing the phone through the wallpapers also fitting the color themes, also with the third-party dynamic symbols which can match your chosen color palette.
- Google's Tensor chip also makes many of the Pixel 7a's AI features very attractive and a big reason to consider the Pixel 7a – or any Pixel for that matter. For example, Magic Eraser works great, and you have access to features like Google Assistant during phone calls to save space and more.
- Generally, this software at the Pixel 7a does the best, appreciation to the performance enhancements Google has offered when talking about the specification. This is quick, approachable also simple in

using. When you are the enthusiast of the stock of Android knowledge, also you cannot move in error with the Pixel 7a.
- The big advantage of choosing the Pixel, of course, is that it's native Google hardware and at the forefront when it comes to software updates. Expect 4 years of software updates on the Pixel 7a and 5 years of security updates - and you'll be the first to get those updates for new versions of Android.
- Furthermore, it is a clutter-free device that offers Google apps and services that are well-integrated for a smooth experience. There aren't many Android phones that have such a clean software experience at this kind of price, so if you enjoy a clean experience without the clutter, then you should definitely look at the Pixel 7a.
- The phone will also be updated with feature drops, where new features are rolling out to Pixel devices. It often introduces something new, often using AI. Through the fundamental hardware being the similar to the power just like the Google's other

gadgets, this has no object there will not be equivalence among the Pixel 7a also other additional costly Pixel gadgets.

Specifications

- Like last year's 6a, the Pixel 7a looks strikingly similar to the standard Pixel 7 and shares its best features – though there are differences that explain the price difference.
- First, the 7a is a bit small. Its 6.1-inch display isn't as large as the 7's 6.3-inch panel, and as a result the phone is slightly lighter overall - albeit by just 4g. It's not as thin as the Pixel 7 at 9mm, but overall it's still pretty sleek and compact.
- The design is otherwise similar to other Pixel 7 phones, though, with a matching camera band on the

back, although it's a little less prominent here. This device has it in four different color selections which are: Charcoal, Snow also the Sea are generally obtainable, and bright Coral is a Google Store exclusive.
- Impressively, the 7a also has an IP67 rating, meaning it's pretty much protected from dust and water damage.
- The screen itself is an OLED panel through the Full HD+ resolution also a 90Hz refresh rate. It's now a same as the regular 7, though to be fair it lags behind the competition: smoother 120Hz screens are now standard on other mid-range phones, though for most people the difference is relatively small.
- The screen includes a fingerprint sensor, but also a selfie camera that allows you to use face unlock. This will not appear astonishing, and the former Pixel the devices have absent the technology (just, indeed, some flagships do come with). However, it's back in the Pixel 7 and 7 Pro, and now it appears to be part of the 7a as well.

- It is important that you know that you know that gadget supported via the Tensor G2, Google's persona in-house chipset which is equally at the two phones Pixel 7 and 7 Pro. At those devices, this is mostly to be the small underpowered than to other flagship selections, and at the 7a, this will give the outstanding power to contest through the mid-range competitors.
- To keep it simple, it only comes in one version: 8GB of RAM and 128GB of storage.
- The camera has also had some upgrades, with a new 64Mp main camera, a 13Mp ultra-wide and a 13Mp selfie camera. These aren't the same cameras found on the other Pixel 7 phones, so it's likely that the 7a will be a little behind them in quality, but all the lenses are higher resolution than the Pixel 6a equivalents, so it should be a recent upgrade year.
- One certain update is the addition of the wireless charging – a first for the Pixel a. It's only a slow 7.5W, but most standard wireless chargers don't go much faster than that anyway. The phone also

- supports 18W wired charging via USB-C, but keep in mind that Google doesn't include a charge in the box.
- As for the battery itself, the 4,385 mAh unit isn't the biggest around, but it's likely enough to get you through the day.
- And finally, the software. You will not astonished to hear the Google device has introduced the Android 13, the newest kind of the operating system. It will also get the same update promise as Google's premium phones, with three major OS updates (ie to Android 16) plus five years of security patches.

Tips and tricks of Google Pixel 7a

Activate Quick Tap

- Google announced the Quick Tap to the Pixel 7a models, allowing this to be just like the nonphysical replacement to the so cherished Active Corner. This does not accurately replace the features that old Pixel fans loved, and this is the simple method to fix additional features on the fingertips.
- Making use of the Quick Touch is just simple as possible. Everything you will perform is to just double-click the back of the gadget to initiate the selected order. This selection are not endless, and you will attempt out diverse specifications such as making a screenshot otherwise introducing the Google Assistant. When you will not see the Quick Tap you want via the Google's prevailing menu, you will likewise be ready to

introduce the application. For instance, you have the Quick Tap set up to unlock the LIFX application therefore you will the access smart lights all through your house.

Take the following steps in setting up the Quick Touch:

- Unlock the settings list.
- Choose the system title.
- Click gestures.
- Select Quick Touch.
- Choose the order.

Permit direct captioning

- Live Caption is among the greatest suitable approachability features at the Google models. This will be the lifesaver at the noise location at a point you will not hear the video, otherwise the silent ones at the

place you do not need to turn up the volume. The AI-driven specification includes the real-time subtitles to almost other media, comprising of the videos, podcasts also authentic phone calls at the Pixel 7a.
- Although you have to search into the settings list for most all of the regulator, live captioning is simple to see through the volume rocker. When you turn the volume up or down, you will view the bubble display through the little text box on the bottommost. This is not checked, and the text box is a live caption toggle.
- Let's say you need additional regulator over the captions. At this case, you will unlock the settings list to control the vulgarity favorites also choose whether the caption comprises of the sound stickers such as laughing also song.

These are steps to be taken in order to view the live caption list:

- Unlock the settings list.

- Select the Accessibility segment.
- Press Live also clasp at that.
- When you have set up Live Caption at the settings list, this is the good knowledge to double-check that through the volume control.

Buying the Google Pixel 7a casing

- The subsequent Google Pixel 7a guideline don't have anything with the software, and this likewise the only specification you will modify before the device get to the door.
- Fortunately, you may have already done the work to see most of the finest casing within. You have frustrated covering numerous groupings, comprising of the slim cases, clear cases, also most battle-tested harsh selections. You will likewise look out for the Google's initial -party silicon case that

follows the similar creativity which begins from the Pixel 7a.

Start playing now

- Chances are you will hear song if you are out also or trying to leave. This will not continually to be the taste, and it has the opportunity this will be the novel artiste you will need to hear. When so, you might try opening the application such as the Shazam to capture the music name, and it comes without assurance you will be fast adequately. In its place, you will attempt the Google's Now Playing specification. This designs the cut just like one of the top Google Pixel 7a guidelines due to the one specification you will use deprived of a second thought.
- Now Playing listens to ambient songs also automatically shows the music, also the artiste at the

bottommost of the screen. This is important, this retains the history of the previous fewer music you have eavesdropped probably you forget to write it down. Now the simplest method to remove playback is to unlock the settings list also type in the search bar. This is likewise concealed beneath the sound and vibration list when you need to clasp that alongside the Live caption.

Register the fingerprints – perhaps two times

- There's something special about setting up a new phone for the first time. Clicking on the power tab also bringing the appearance to life is exciting, it doesn't matter on how frequently you perform that. This comes with a lot list to make use of also settings to personalize, though the setup procedure will be frustrating at times. Through that in your mind, there are some Google Pixel 7a guidelines also understanding to try also that will design the device be the best.

Activate Quick Tap

- Google announced the Quick Tap to the Pixel 7a models, allowing that to work like the nonphysical replacement to the very –cherished Active Edge. This doesn't precisely replace the features that old Pixel aficionados loved, and this is the simple method to bring additional specifications close to you.
- Making use of the Quick Touch is just simple as possible. Everything you will have to perform is to double-tap the back of the gadget to initiate the selected order. This selections are not endless, and you will attempt out diverse specifications such as the making the screenshot otherwise introducing Google Assistant.

When you cannot see the Quick Tap you need through the Google's prevailing menu, you will likewise that to introduce the application. For instance, you get the Quick Tap set up to unlock the LIFX application therefore you will have right to the smart lights all through the house.

At this point this is the methods to set up the Quick Touch:

- Unlock the settings list.
- Choose the system title.
- Click gestures.
- Select Quick Touch.
- Choose the order.

Enable Live Caption

- Live Caption is among the greatest suitable approachability features at the Google lineup. This will be the lifesaver at the noisy atmosphere the place you cannot hear the video, otherwise the quiet one the place you do not desire to turn up the volume. The AI-driven specifications includes real-time subtitles to almost every media, comprising of the videos, podcasts also the real phone calls at the Pixel 7a.

- Although you will dig into the settings list for virtually all the regulators, live captioning is the simple to see through the volume rocker. When you turn the volume up or down, you will view the bubble display through the little text box on the bottommost. This is not checked, and the text box is a live caption clasp.
- Let's say you need additional regulator against the captions. At this case, you will unlock the settings list to control the vulgarity favorites also choose whether the caption comprises of the sound stickers such as laughing also song.

These are the methods to search for the live caption list:

- Unlock the settings list.
- Select the Accessibility segment.
- Click on the Live also fastening on that.
- When you have the set up Live Caption at the settings list, this is the good knowledge to double-check that through the volume control.

Purchasing the Google Pixel 7a casing

- On the subsequent Google Pixel 7a guideline never had anything in connection with the software, and this is likewise the only specification that you will modify prior to the arrival of the gadget to the door.

Start playing now

- Chances are you will be hearing the music if you are outside or around. This will not constantly be to the desire, and it will create the time this will be the novel artiste you need to hear. When so, you might try opening the application such as the Shazam to capture the music name, and this has doesn't come with an assurance you will be fast adequately. In its place, you will attempt the Google's Now Playing specifications. This designs the cut just like one of the top Google Pixel 7a guidelines due to the one specification you will use deprived of a second thought.
- Now Playing eavesdrops to ambient songs also automatically shows the music also artiste on the bottommost of the screen. The most important, this retains the account of the previously some music you have eavesdropped perhaps you didn't remember to write that down. Now the simplest method to remove playback is to unlock the settings list also type in the search bar. This is likewise concealed beneath the sound and

vibration list when you need to fast that alongside the Live caption.

Register your fingerprints - maybe twice

- You can bet the Pixel 7a's fingerprint indicator isn't the identical one that was found in the in the Pixel 6, and this is continuously the best to be vigilant. Google's flagships have been riddled through some problems, not at the point registering fingerprints, to slow unlocking, also likewise in the crashing when the battery dies. Therefore, after this know other issues with the Pixel 7a, and the finest method to upsurge the unlocking probabilities is to enroll back the fingerprints. Its sensor location is very simple to locate, subsequently this will be the best awareness of registering all the thumbs two times.

Take the following steps in setting up your Google pixel 7a:

- Go to settings.
- Go to Fingerprint Unlocking.
- Log in the PIN if you are notify.
- Choose include all the fingerprint.
- Taking the procedures to scan the whole fingerprint.

Setting up the individual security specifications

- Even if you are an adrenaline junkie otherwise merely traveling, this is the best to get the planning just if there is an accident. Google's individual Safety application puts almost all the things on emergency contacts, medical data, also individual information such as the address—in one suitable place. The data you logged will then be stored locally on the gadget.

- Personal Security first asks you to add emergency contacts that people can contact in a situation of emergency deprived of opening the Pixel 7a. Different medical data lists allow you to include all the things through the blood type to dislikes also medicines, when you are taking them.
- At this point, you will go from the security checking's at the phone the device can alert you on a definite time also initiate the emergency share when you do not answer — otherwise initiate the emergency share, that will make announcements of the place with the push of the tab. individual Safety likewise backs car accident detection with the alerts about close natural catastrophes with the emergencies.

Check the spam call

- The Spam call are widespread, but a lot individual of individual wanting to contact you concerning extending the vehicle warranty does not look like that going to decrease any time soon. The FCC with the entirely three foremost US carriers has introduced methods to fight spam, and this is coming all the time—virtually such as calls at inside the home. Fortunately, Google is creating the steps to prevent unsolicited robocalls.
- When you unlock the device application also go to Settings (the three-dot list in the topmost-right side), you will see another Pixel 7a guideline. This is named Spam also Call Screen also lives beneath the Help header. If you unlock that, you will have access to toggles which will recognize caller ID also spam, enable verified calls, and also fine-tune Call Screen settings. Confirmed calls show the caller ID also the purpose for the incoming calls when this through a business.
- When you go to the Call Screen list, this can it will offer you the selections to automatically combat spam. You will sieve out

disbelieved spam also perhaps fake numbers through one click, also it comes with a lot of selections for taking care of the initial -time callers also private otherwise hidden the numbers.

Adjust your keyboard settings

- The Pixel 7a is very simple in using the through the one hand compare to other Pixel 7 sibling. Nevertheless, most times you still desire to tweak things at this point also at that point makes the life simpler. It's suggested to resize the Pixel 7's keyboard in making that simpler to have, and in this Pixel 7a guideline is to personalize all the thing else.
- You will see the Pixel 7a's keyboard settings beneath the Languages & Inputs list. At this point, you will

turn Google Voice Typing on or off, otherwise go in to Gboard's settings for the small additional power. Gboard allows you to include language favorites (also dissimilar keyboards through default characters), enable swipe typing when you do not need to lift the finger, also including the terms to the individual dictionary. This is the simplest method to battle the autocorrect problems, and you will likewise tell Gboard to forget the words also information you've learned if you want to start over.

Try the material yourself

- Introduced with Android 12, Material You aims to make the device just like important like imaginable. This gives a sequence of personalized selections through the application symbols to the

widgets, every of the themed round the background
- This is simple sufficient to regulate the colorful Android knowledge by long pressing at the background. It can unlock the list through the selections for wallpaper with the style, widgets and home settings. When you need color-coordinated application symbols you will see them beneath the initial selection, and be aware which of the specification is mostly restricted to Google's initial -party applications. Widgets are in the similar boat— Google's selection gives diverse shapes with colors, although the most third-party making are restricted to classic rectangles.
- You will see the greatest freedom at the Google Pictures widget that have been talked about before. Before you upgrade to version 5.65, you will view like half a dozen frame shapes with the sizes to selected through.

Personalize the Quick Settings

- By Chances one will see himself or herself in the Pixel 7a's quick settings list even if it is one time in a day. Even if you are turning on Bluetooth, the favorite Wi-Fi network, otherwise initiating a battery saver, this retains the essential functions in one swipe. Although you can try pulling down the shade also swiping left otherwise right to access every selection, this is very simple to personalize the menu. You moved specifications such as the airplane mode at the first page and settings such as the auto-rotate to the next page due to you might or will not make use that.
- When you have not modernized the Quick Settings, you will not realize how easy that is. In its place of pursuing for a partition, what you need to perform is to click at the pencil which is on the bottommost of the list. You will then move also keep the current tiles also include novel ones through the selected third-party applications.
- Nothing like the third-party tiles just like widgets, and you have

included the capability to design the novel asana job with the click of the tab, therefore you will not have to chase down the editor for not remembering.

Tap quickly to make the screenshot

- The default method to make the screenshot at Android is to hold down two tabs (usually the power and volume buttons). However, the layout of the buttons can be tricky. Google has revealed the screenshots of the rear touchscreen on the Pixel 6. The Pixel 7a shares this gesture.

To use it, follow these steps:

- Go to Settings > System.
- Tap gestures

- Select a quick tap to initiate actions.
- On the next screen, enable Quick Touch. The first action to take a screenshot is selected by default.
- Once installed, double-tap the back of the phone to take a screenshot.
- Choose the suitable selection when you choose the diverse purpose, like the playing/pausing media otherwise introducing Google Assistant. If you accidentally activate the double-tap feature, you can disable it by selecting the option to request a stronger tap.

Multilingual keyboard

- If you are an expert linguist who is fluent in different languages, you may want to consider installing a bilingual or multilingual keyboard. When typing continuously, this eliminates the need to switch back and forth between languages. How to do this:

- Go to Settings > System.
- Tap Languages and input.
- Tap the on-screen keyboard
- Select Gboard.
- Tap the languages.
- Tap Add keyboard.
- Select a language from the list.
- Make sure multilingual typing is enabled and complete the setup.
- Now, instead of manually switching between languages before typing, the keyboard will do it for you and suggest relevant words and spelling corrections.

Turn it off at a glance

- Unlike the previous sentences, this involves deactivating something. Google's At-a-glance widget is a handy tool that automatically displays your Gmail account's weather conditions, important calendar events, travel plans, and more. It's on by default on Pixel smartphones, but you can turn it off if you find it annoying.

At this point this is the method to use in turning that off at a look:

- Long press the widget and tap Customize.
- Select at a glance from the list
- Tap Turn off.
- Disabling at first glance will not free up space for other widgets or app icons. This likewise fades out through the home also lock screens.

Allow home screen rotation

- By default, you use the smartphone's tall, dim screen in portrait orientation, switching to landscape for games or the camera app. It is not necessary. Pixel 6a's home screen can be rotated to landscape mode.
- Tap on home settings after long pressing on wallpaper. Toggle Allow home screen rotation.

Enable direct captioning

- Direct captioning is useful, whether for accessibility or in noisy environments. Google's artificial intelligence and research data generate text for videos, podcasts, audio messages and phone calls.
- The Pixel 6a's volume control has access to Live Caption. A small bubble appears when you press the volume button to adjust it. At this point you will switch that on otherwise off.

- If you can't see the volume when you press the buttons or want to adjust it, go to Settings > Accessibility and tap the Live caption.

Quickly turn off access to the microphone or camera

- Google's Android releases emphasize privacy. Android 11 added one-time permissions for location, microphone, and camera. Android 12 added icons for when apps use the camera or microphone. Android 13 extended the discretion dashboard to seven days via 24 hours.
- Google has added one-touch switches to mute the microphone and camera. Drop down the Quick Settings shade and tap on Tiles.

Making the fingerprint sensor additional trustworthy

- The fingerprint sensor at the Pixel 7a is not astonishing, therefore when you need to create that little additional trustworthy, it comes with the convenient guideline through the back if the iPhone TouchID sensors were not very hot: just registering the similar finger otherwise thumbs numerous occasions.
- After setting up the initial fingerprint scan, move to the Settings > Security > Fingerprint opening. All you need is to enter the PIN to access settings. Click "Add Fingerprint" also scan the similar finger otherwise the thumb once more. This will make the scanner to reduce probable of crashing.

Tap back to make the screenshot

- For times, the default method inn taking the screenshot at the Android was to click at the two tabs collectively. This will be the bit confusing pending on the location also the layout of the tabs. And you will allow the gesture in taking the screenshot through just clicking at the back of the device.
- Unlock the Settings > System also presently chose the "Gestures". On the top right, you will view "Quick Touch". Choose the selection also fastening on the specification on the other screen. Through the default the action that is set
- Screenshot therefore presently if you double click at the back of the device that will take the screenshot.
- When you had moderately get another purpose, you will perform so, maybe this is stopping otherwise playing songs, introducing the Google Assistant, otherwise displaying notifications.
- When you see that very simple to initiate the double-pressing specification, you will fastening the selection at the bottommost of the

screen to require a stronger tap to activate the feature of your choice.

One hand mode

- The Pixel 7a has large screens, therefore you will see that difficulty to attain. Which is the reason of the Android 12 current comes with the one-handed mode that will takes things down through the topmost of the screen.
- Move to the Settings
- System
- Gestures and select "One-handed mode".
- Presently turn that on. When you activated, swiping down from the bottommost of the screen will take down the operator interface, permitting you to access items at the topmost through the thumb.

Switch off "at a glance"

- Through the default, the Pixel home screen has something named "at a glance" on the topmost. In virtually all the cases that will show weather conditions, and that will likewise automatically show a significant schedule
- Occasions with the travelling strategies that come through the Gmail account.
- When you need to turn that off, the only thing you will do is to long-press the At-a-glance widget also click the Customize. Presently press on "At a Glance" menu also then "Disable". You will likewise permit otherwise deactivate the display of precise specifications there.

Permit the home screen rotation

- When you want to be using the device at the landscape orientation, the Pixel coming with the home screen rotation specification switched off through the default can be a little annoying, and luckily you will turn that on.
- Long click at the background of the home screen also click on "General Settings". Presently fastening the switch that is the bottommost close to "Allow home screen rotation". But presently, when you flip the home screen to landscape, the interface moves through you. All you need do is to certain to turn on the "Auto-Rotate" specification at the Quick Settings shade to ensure you will not have to tap the small rotating symbol at the screen always.

Wireless charging

- The Pixel's reverse wireless charging is named Battery Share, but this lets you charge well-matched gadgets wirelessly from the back of the device. You only pull down the fast settings shade also press on the battery sharing selection. Move the device over also keep a compatible wireless charging product at its back.
- Likewise, when you long click the battery sharing symbol, you will get the major battery sharing settings. At this point you will see the slider which permits you to set the boundary for if to pause charging. Maybe when you are charging the favorite buds otherwise smartwatch drained the device battery. Modify the slider till this boundary is on the comfy level. The default is only 10 percent.

Speedily go to Google Pay through the lock screen

- When you have set up Google Pay for contactless payments, you'll be able to access that straight through your lock screen. If the device is unlocked, you will view the small card symbol in the bottommost right corner of the screen. Click on it to quickly launch GPay therefore you will be using that to pay for services.
- When this is not there, make sure Google Pay is set to the selection of the card but currently move to Settings > Display > Lock screen also be certain you have turned on the "Show wallet" switch.

Multilingual keyboard

- When you speak additional compare to one language also use them frequently, a bilingual or multilingual keyboard will probably come in handy. Instead of constantly switching among languages

- Move to Settings > System > Languages > On-Screen Keyboard also presently click at the 'Gboard'. Presently press on Languages also "Add Keyboard" also select among of the languages from the list.
- Now if you have started typing, the mounted keyboard can automatically recognize if you are typing on one otherwise another also will accurate also envisage the spelling of the two deprived of getting to manually switch.

Speedily turn off access to the microphone or camera

- It's really fast, and this is the novel specification. Drop down into the settings shade also see the camera likewise the microphone toggle. Press once also that will instantaneously lock the camera also microphone therefore that no apps at the device will be access them.

Now playing history

- Among the Pixel's greatest important specifications at the current years is showing the title also artiste of other music presently playing at the place that you are. In other to allow that go to Settings > Display > Lock screen & Now playing also fastening the switch when this is never already at the point.
- In other see recently tagged music, move down to "Now Playing History" also you will view the menu of music, including the period they were labelled. Moreover, when you need to include the shortcut to the menu, you will. Of a truth, when you are on the menu, the popup will appear asking when you need to. Only press "Yes".

- When this is not there, move to the Home screen, long-click on the wallpaper, also press Widgets at the pop-up list. Presently select Android System Intelligence also click then press the Now Playing History shortcut also move that to the space at the home screen.

Disable the Google Discover page

- From the left of the home screen you will virtually and continuously see the Google Feed page, which will show the news also the videos that contemplates to be significant to you, and you will turn that off. Only long click at the wallpaper also select "Main setting". Currently switch off "move to the access Google application".

Display the RAW image switcher in camera

- When you need a handbook adjust to select among the RAW and JPE, you will get one. Unlock the camera, click on the settings button at the side also presently select "More settings". Now select "Advanced" also fastening the selection which say "RAW+JPEG" regulate.
- If you unlock the camera settings list which loads in the viewfinder/monitor view, you will currently view the selection which allows you switch among RAW+JPEG otherwise only shoot JPEG.

Android 12 Easter Eggs

- This is not the novel type of Android deprived of the Easter egg,

also the route to see that is the similar just like the continuously. Unlock Settings > about device also click type. At the following screen, click "Android version" repeatedly till the clock widget picture loads.
- Presently, let the minute hand until the time reaches 12 o'clock. This will help load to patch Android 12 easter egg at the device theme colors.
- The Easter egg also has one extra element: long-click the home screen also press Widgets. Presently select "Android S Widget" also move also dropping the Paint chip shortcut to the home screen. When you need, you will reshape the widget to display numerous color cards. Press that also it will load complete screen also you will click other personal card to share the suit. This is of no importance, and this is the Easter egg, this wouldn't needing the period.